i

Thank you for your support,

Ronald Lucas

I DON'T WANT TO BE A MILLIONAIRE;

I JUST WANT TO LIVE LIKE ONE!

RONALD G. LUCAS, SR

This is a work of creative nonfiction. Some names characters, places, and incidents may have been fictionalized for in varying degrees, for varying purposes.

First edition October 2021

ISBN 978-1-68524-437-8 (ebook)

ISBN 978-1-68524-438-5 (paperback)

Published by Bookbaby

FOREWARD

Some might say he could squeeze a penny so hard that George Washington would holler; but that was my friend, Ronald George Lucas. Luke is what I called him. In the spring of 1958, I met Luke when he moved next door to me on Holbrook Street, NE in Washington, DC. I was one year ahead of him in school but when we formed our high school fraternity, he was the one we elected to handle our money. Later as young adults when we formed a social club, he again was our treasurer and financial guru. In March of 1965, when I got married, he was my best man. After he graduated from Howard University and started work at the Federal Power Commission, he was elected to the Board of Directors of his agency's credit union. Later he became treasurer of the board and he mentioned some of the challenges of that job and these challenges were amazing. These challenges included flight from the credit union because of minority participation on the board of directors. As treasurer, he paid the credit union bills and participated in setting interest rates on loans and on customer accounts. Also, he participated in choosing investments that met the requirements of the National Credit Union Administration (NCUA). In the face of declining deposits, he worked on reducing expenses by moving outsourced computer account services to in house. Despite these efforts, the NCUA decided that Luke's credit union was too small to offer the variety of services available at many credit unions. Merger with a larger credit union was recommended. Luke worked on merging his credit union with the Ft Belvoir Federal Credit Union. Luke's experience as treasurer taught him the inner workings of financial institutions and how to budget, invest and maintain and prepare payroll.

Later, I introduced him to Grace United Church in Takoma Park, MD where he initially took his kids to Sunday School, but later joined himself. His participation at church grew as he became member at large of the finance committee, next chairman of the church counsel, then treasurer and finally chair of the finance committee. During his time as treasurer, he oversaw the sale of the church's parsonage and using his credit union experience in selecting safe investments, he persuaded the finance committee to invest in a real estate fund before that market exploded. That fund allowed the church to replace its heating system and its entire roof with the investment gains. The principle of the investment was never touched.

In 1992, Luke and a couple of families bought VIP Travel Agency Greenbelt, MD. Soon after, Luke became president and steered the agency through the difficult times of airlines no longer paying agency commissions, increasing competition from online travel booking sites and competition from larger agencies. Most recently with the COVID-19 pandemic crippling the travel industry for nearly a year and a half now, Luke has kept his agency afloat.

In the past, Luke has said that he did _not_ want to be a millionaire but wanted to live like one. So, writing a book with this title is appropriate. His unique experiences make him qualified to share "**BBS**" – **B**udgeting, **S**aving and **S**pending which he talks a lot about in this book.

This book is enlightening to many, both young and old.

With some help for the intimate details of Luke's experiences, Lawrence B. Herbert, Sr., Lifelong friend

Lawrence B. Herbert, Sr.

THIS BOOK IS DEDICATED TO MY WIFE,
MALCINE; MY CHILDREN, DANA, DEREK,
RONALD, CHUCK; MY GRANDCHILDREN;
MY MOM WHO TAUGHT ME TO SAVE;
MY EXTENDED FAMILY AND FRIENDS

Table of Contents

INTRODUCTION

"Therefore if you have not been faithful in the unrighteous mammon (wealth), who will commit to your trust the true riches?" Luke 16:11, NKJV. "And you shall remember the Lord your God, for it is He who gives you power to get wealth, that He may establish His covenant which He swore to your fathers, as it is this day." Deuteronomy 8:18, NKJV. "I can do all things through Christ who strengthens me." Philippians 4:13, NKJV.

Through Christ, I can be disciplined to budget, save, spend and manage debt while recognizing that not by my strength, but by His, I can live large and understand that if I can be wise with a little, He will trust me with much.

"I DON'T WANT TO BE A MILLIONAIRE; I JUST WANT TO LIVE LIKE ONE" is a book about a lifestyle which can be obtained through having plans with achievable goals and having discipline to execute those plans. The first three chapters describe "**BSS**" - plans for **B**udgeting, **S**aving and **S**pending. Setting money aside and purchasing are discussed in multiple chapters to reinforce budgeting, saving and spending before the text turns to dealing with credit card debt. Finally, retirement is examined with a final thought of living large – not being a millionaire but living like one.

"For the love of money is a root of all *kinds of* evil, for which some have strayed from the faith in their greediness, and pierced themselves through with many sorrows." 1 Timothy 6:10, NKJV.

Chapter I

Budgeting

What I Earn

Earnings are paid wages for labor or services. They are not casino winnings, the lotto, number hits, bonuses, gifts, loan repayments or found money. If you worked for it, you have earned it. Work is necessary. Second Thessalonians 3:10, NKJV states "For even when we were with you, we commanded you this: If anyone will not work, neither shall he eat." We work to have earnings and with earnings on the regular, we can set a budget. Setting a budget requires examining earnings after deductions such as taxes, social security, Medicare and allotments like retirement, health care, savings, childcare and other things. By the grace of God, we hope that earnings will grow over time. Therefore, we should look at earnings in phases.

Phase 1 Earnings – Just Entering the Workforce

As a young person, before your first real job, you have a limited awareness of how much you need to earn to sustain your desired lifestyle. "I want my own car; I want my own place." Okay, with a car, you will need to pay a car note, insurance, gas, maintenance and repairs. Having my own place will likely mean having your own apartment. With that, you will need to pay rent, electricity, cable, internet, condo fees and more. Some apartment managers will not accept your application unless your monthly salary is three times the cost of your rent. These are your basic expenses, the cost of which will determine your lifestyle and going beyond a car and an apartment, you will need probably to earn 3.5 to 4 times the sum of these basic expenses to survive minimally. For example, you want a new Toyota Camry and you can get one at a total cost of $27,000 including taxes, tags, title and dealer costs. For a 60-month term loan, monthly payments are a little more than $490.00 at a 3.5% interest rate. If the apartment you want rents for $1300.00 per month, the basic expense for this new car and apartment lifestyle is $1790.00 per month. Your salary should at least be $6,265.00 per month or $75,180.00 per year after taxes and other deductions. According to National Association of Colleges and Employers, the average starting salary for a college graduate is $50,944.00 in 2019. Obviously, if you are just starting out, expectation of this lifestyle is set to high based on your just entering the workforce.

Phase 2 Earnings – Midcareer Employment

Midcareer employment is that period between being no longer a probationary employee, but a permanent employee and being retired. Midcareer employment can also be that period between no longer being an apprentice, but a craftsman starting his or her own business; and being retired. Ideally, this is a period of growth in earnings because this period is likely to be one of growing expenses. Continuing the example from the previous paragraph, you lowered your expectations, bought a used car costing $275.00 per month and got a roommate to split the expenses for your now not-so-high-scaled apartment choice costing $1100.00 per month. Now your basic expenses total $825.00 ($275 + $1100/2) per month and applying the formula for minimal income, your salary needs to be $2887.50 per month or $34,650.00 per year. Now if you are a college grad making the average starting salary, you are in the game.

The next question is how much I will earn until I retire. The Association of Public & Land-Grant Universities presents the following:

Return on Investment: Lifetime Earnings by Level of Education

- High School Diploma - $1,304,000
- Some College - $1,547,000
- Associate degree - $1,727,000
- Bachelor's degree - $2,268,000
- Advanced degree - $2,671,000

Over a 30-year career, the growth in earnings will vary based on level of education. "The Hamilton Project – Median Annual Earnings over Career" graphs earnings at the start of a career and the following table is a partial extraction of the information on the graph:

	Annual Earnings in Thousands of 2014 Dollars from Start of Career						
	0 Year	5 Years	10 Years	15 Years	20 Years	25 Years	30 Years
High School Degree or GED	$8	$18	$23	$27	$30	$32	$33
Some College No Degree	$11	$21	$29	$34	$37	$39	$39
Associate Degree	$16	$28	$36	$40	$43	$43	$45
College Degree All Majors	$21	$41	$51	$56	$60	$62	$61

While earnings are anticipated to grow during the period of Midcareer employment, so will expenses. The cost of a car and a place to live will increase due to inflation, while other expenses such as starting a family will also appear. The importance of choosing a career with a great growth potential is paramount. Choosing a career is also a subject of such great importance that it requires separate study and analysis apart from this presentation and for the sake of brevity will not be discussed in this book.

Phase 3 Earnings – Retirement

Everyone should plan for retirement. If a class on retirement is available, that class should be taken 2 to 5 years before retiring. Continuing to work part time or full should be an option and not a necessity during retirement. Earnings in retirement will likely be less than earnings during the last year of employment. Preparation for retirement is critical. How have you protected earnings during the previous phase of life? Is your house paid off or close to being paid off? What about other major expenses? Did you replace your roof or central AC unit before retiring? Are your kids out of school and no more tuitions are due? How will life be for you earning 50 to 65% less than your earnings in the last year before retirement? Chapter VII will continue later a discussion of retirement.

What I Spend

The adage that "the more you make, the more you spend" has a ring of truth but you don't need necessarily to spend more. How about make more, spend the same or less according to a budget. Buying something because it is on sale does not save money if you don't need the item. How about trying to wait to buy something you need until it is on sale and spending for it as you planned per a budget. Just as earnings were examined in phases, so can spending be looked at in the same way.

Phase 1 Spending – Just Entering the Workforce

Since we cannot always pay cash for stuff, establishing credit is extremely important. You have control of your future credit profile because you have no credit history. Some ways to have a good credit profile are:

- If your parents are responsible with their credit cards by paying their bills on time and not maxing out their cards, **be an authorized user** on your parents' credit card. You don't need to use their card but you will benefit from their good credit history just by having your name on their account.
- Obtain a **secured credit card**. A secured credit care is a credit card that you put down a deposit to get approval and you can charge up to your deposit amount on that card. The credit limit on this type of card is generally low. It offers the experience of having a credit card but limits the risks of overspending.
- **Pay your balance in full each month.** For most people, this is a challenge; however, this practice eliminates finance charges. Also, it shows discipline, reliability, commitment and credit worthiness.
- **Upgrade to a traditional credit card.** Often after proving yourself with a secured credit card for six months to a year, you can possibly upgrade to a traditional credit card with a higher limit and not dependent on a deposit to secure the card. At this point, it is important to try to avoid carrying a balance and to pay all of your bills on time. Avoiding carrying a balance (pay your balance in full each month) eliminates the trap of increasing debt and growing finance charges. Increasing debt obligates future earnings. Paying all bills on time builds good credit. Paying bills on time is not limited to credit card bills, but it is important to pay all bills on time, such as paying rent, doctor bills, utilities and student loans because they all become part of your credit history. If one is left unpaid and goes into default, that negative report stays on your credit history for seven years. Unlike other debt, student loans are not likely to be discharge through bankruptcy, a final declaration of not being able to pay bills.

Phase 2 Spending – Midcareer Employment

As mentioned before, Midcareer Employment is that period between being a permanent, non-probationary employee and being retired. With earnings on the regular, you spend in proportion to a salary expected to increase over time. Spending increases over time also as responsibilities increase. Spending may start out for just you with a car and a place to live. Marriage may come along and now there are two persons in the picture, maybe followed by children. It becomes even more important to list expenses. Those expenses should also include consideration for health care, retirement and life insurance which may be part of an employment agreement. Treat savings like an expense. On a regular basis for savings, have a set amount to go into a separate account from the account used to pay bills.

Phase 3 Spending - Retirement

In retirement, spending should be less, and the peak of spending should have been during Phase 2 – Midcareer Employment. If you have a family, the hope is that kids are through with school and out on their own. Hopefully, your home is paid off or close to being paid off. The list of expenses in Phase 2 should have decreased. Spending in retirement should not require a second job. A second or part time job should be an option and not a necessity.

My Budget

Since failure to plan is a plan to fail, "My Budget" is a plan to succeed. Budgeting is a continuous process of planning and monitoring, no matter the phase of life. Creating a budget based on expenses 15 to 20% below your after taxes take-home pay works in all phases as well. In Phase 1 Just entering the workforce, income and expenses are little. In Phase 2 Midcareer Employment, both income and expenses are dynamic and expanding. In Phase 3 Retirement, both income and expenses are less than in the previous phase.

What does "My Budget" look like? Maybe like this:

My Budget - My Money							
Month 1				Month 2			
Description	Date	Amount	Balance	Description	Date	Amount	Balance
Take-home Pay	1/1/2021	$2,500.00	$2,500.00	Take-home Pay	2/1/2021	$2,500.00	$2,500.00
				Left month before		$1,050.00	$3,550.00
Fixed Expense				Fixed Expense			
Description	Date	Amount	Balance	Description	Date	Amount	Balance
rent	1/4/2021	$550.00	$1,950.00	car	2/4/2021	$550.00	$3,000.00
car	1/12/2021	$275.00	$1,675.00	rent	2/12/2021	$275.00	$2,725.00
Variable Expense				Variable Expense			
Description	Date	Amount	Balance	Description	Date	Amount	Balance
Groceries	1/5/2021	$250.00	$1,425.00	Groceries	2/6/2021	$180.00	$2,545.00
Groceries	1/19/2021	$300.00	$1,125.00	Groceries	2/15/2021	$220.00	$2,325.00
Gas	1/5/2021	$40.00	$1,085.00	Gas	2/3/2021	$42.00	$2,283.00
Gas	1/12/2021	$35.00	$1,050.00	Gas	2/10/2021	$40.00	$2,243.00
Left at end of month			$1,050.00	Left at end of month			$2,243.00

Don't be overwhelmed by numbers. It is just simple addition and subtraction. In this example, a framework is established for a pattern of controlled financial freedom based on earned income and four expenses which of course, will be more than four for most people. Notice that the expenses are separated into fixed and variable expenses. A fixed expense is usually a reoccurring expense that is for each month due the same amount and due on a same date. A variable expense is an expense that will vary on the amount and the date of the expense. A budget should identify these expenses. On the chart above, if there are more items, add lines to accommodate those items. The math is simple. In Month 1, start with income, $2500.00

and subtract the first fixed expense rent, $550.00 to get a balance, $1950.00. Subtract the next fixed expense, car expense, $275.00 from the previous balance, $1950.00 to get a balance, $1675.00. Follow this pattern with other fixed expenses such as a credit card, cell phone and even savings to a separate account different from the account used to pay bills. These fixed expenses are those reoccurring expenses that if missed will carry a consequence like a late fee and a negative impact on credit scores. While including savings as a fixed expense will not incur these negative marks, treating savings as being important as a fixed expense is a good way to start building a solid financial base.

In the example in the first month, $1675.00 is left after fixed expenses were paid. Subtract groceries, $250.00 from $1675.00 to get a balance of $1425.00 which is reduced when $300 of more groceries is subtracted to get a balance of $1125.00. While necessary, groceries can be budgeted more or less in amount and frequency. Add other variable expenses such as entertainment, eating out, personal expenses and follow the same pattern of subtracting expenses from the previous balance. The good part is that if you have budgeted well, there will be money left over to carry forward to the next month. As you can see, $1050.00 was left at the end of Month 1 and now it is available along with take home pay, $2500.00 to have a total of $3550.00 to pay bills in Month 2.

What About Church?

"Honor the Lord with your possessions, and with the firstfruits of all your increase;" Proverbs 3:9, NKJV. Personally, I give a tenth of my earnings to my church. In other words, I tithe.

"Bring all the tithes into the storehouse, that there may be food in My house, and try Me now in this,' says the Lord of hosts, 'If I will not open for you the windows of heaven and pour out for you such blessing that there will not be room enough to receive it." Malachi 3:10, NKJV.

Although not shown in the budget above, giving to church is not a bill and not an expense. It is a cheerful donation from the top of all that you receive (increase) and your walk with God should determine what that donation should be. "So let each one give as he purposes in his heart, not grudgingly or of necessity; for God loves a cheerful giver." 2 Corinthians 9:7, NKJV.

Chapter II.

Savings

Allotments

An allotment is an allocation of something to someone or something. By withholding part of employees' salaries, employers allocate employees' gross salary to the Internal Revenue Service, Social Security Administration, a savings account and other places. Emphasis in this discussion is on an allotment as a direct deposit of funds to a financial institution. Through their payroll office, employers arrange withholdings for Federal Tax, State Tax, Social Security, Medicare, Life Insurance and Health Insurance. By creating a savings allotment, an employer can routinely withhold for deposit a predetermined fixed amount allowing the employee to save without thinking about saving. Employers can arrange direct deposit of pay to a checking account and an allotment to a savings account. Savings taken off the top is now as important as withholding for government purposes (taxes, social security, etc.) and personal needs (health insurance, life insurance, retirement, etc.) and it should be.

Pay Me First

If your employer cannot do allotments to savings, consider "Pay Me First." "Pay Me First" is depositing your entire take-home pay into an interest-bearing savings account and transferring money to a checking account as needed to pay bills. In the previous paragraph on Allotments, the gross salary is allocated to various places such as the Internal Revenue Service, Social Security Administration, a savings account and other places. The remainder after this allocation is net pay or take-home pay which is deposited directly to a financial institution by the employer or handed or mailed to the employee. In this section on "Pay Me First," there is no allotment to savings but a deposit of the entire take-home check to savings.

In Chapter I, the importance of budgeting was discussed. The chart in Chapter I, "My Budget – My Money," can be used to create a "Pay Me First" chart. Below, the chart "My Budget – My Money" has been converted to a "Pay Me First" chart. The components of income and expenses are the same, but now rearranged for "Pay Me First."

The first step in creating a "Pay Me First" chart is to choose a bank or a credit union to open a checking account and a savings account where money can be easily moved from savings to checking. Later in this section, differences in saving accounts will be discussed. Second, arrange for your entire take home pay to be directly deposited into savings. The third step is to list expenses in chronological order. The fourth step is to group expenses into two, three or four amounts which then will equal the amount to be withdrawn from savings.

In the example below, expenses for Month 1 were rent, car note, two trips to the grocery store and 2 gas fill-ups. Based on chronological order, rent and the first trip to the grocery store and gas station were grouped and car note and the second trip to the grocery store and gas station were grouped. Group 1 expenses totaled $840.00 and Group 2 expenses totaled $610.00. The deposit to savings on the first of the month was $2500.00 take-home pay from which $840.00 was withdrawn from savings and deposited to checking on the first and $610.00 was withdrawn from savings and deposited to checking on day twelve. In this example, $1050.00 was left in savings after expenses for Month 1 and available for expenses in Month 2. This chart serves as a template for more expenses which most people will likely have.

Pay Me First							
Month 1				**Month 2**			
Savings Account				**Savings Account**			
Description	Date	Amount	Balance	Description	Date	Amount	Balance
Take-home Pay	1/1/2021	$2,500.00	$2,500.00	Left from previous month		$1,050.00	$1,050.00
Deposit to Savings	1/1/2021	$2,500.00	$2,500.00	Take-home Pay	2/1/2021	$2,500.00	$3,550.00
Withdrawal from Savings	1/1/2021	$840.00	$1,660.00	Withdrawal from Savings	2/1/2021	$772.00	$2,778.00
Withdrawal from Savings	1/12/2021	$610.00	$1,050.00	Withdrawal from Savings	2/10/2021	$535.00	$2,243.00
Checking Account				**Checking Account**			
Description	Date	Amount	Balance	Description	Date	Amount	Balance
Starting Balance	1/1/2021		$50.00	Starting Balance	2/1/2021		$50.00
Deposit to Checking	1/1/2021	$840.00	$890.00	Deposit to Checking	2/1/2021	$772.00	$822.00
Rent	1/4/2021	$550.00	$340.00	rent	2/4/2021	$550.00	$272.00
Groceries	1/5/2021	$250.00	$90.00	gas	2/3/2021	$42.00	$230.00
Gas	1/5/2021	$40.00	$50.00	groceries	2/6/2021	$180.00	$50.00
Deposit to Checking	1/12/2021	$610.00	$660.00	Deposit to Checking	2/10/2021	$495.00	$545.00
Gas	1/12/2021	$35.00	$625.00	gas	2/10/2021	$40.00	$505.00
Car	1/12/2021	$275.00	$350.00	car	2/12/2021	$275.00	$230.00
Groceries	1/19/2021	$300.00	$50.00	groceries	2/15/2021	$180.00	$50.00

Some interest-bearing savings accounts limit the number of withdrawals from savings account to six a month, so payments are put in chronological order and grouped. If you are allowed only six withdrawals a month, you should not withdraw money from savings immediately when each bill due. Instead, sum the bills into three or four amounts. Then plan to pay the three or four amounts with three or four withdrawals from savings. If withdrawals are capped at six each month, you then have two or three opportunities to withdraw in an emergency. For most savings accounts which limit the number of withdrawals, a customer can go above that limit but the customer will be charged a fee.

In the past when interest rates on accounts were higher, interest-bearing savings accounts had greater significance. Financial institutions offered Money Market Accounts which paid higher interest than regular savings and checking accounts. Money Market Accounts sometimes required higher minimum balances and restricted the number of withdrawals as described in the previous paragraph. Today, some banks offer special savings accounts with better interest rates than the interest rates for regular savings accounts. While some banks offer regular savings accounts with interest rates a fraction of a percent, online-savings-accounts may offer interest rates of a half of a percent for high balance accounts. An online-savings-account is a remote savings account usually accessed online and not in person. Current rates are down from the rates offered when online-savings-accounts were first introduced. Research is necessary to find the savings institution, bank or Credit Union which works best for you.

Chapter III.

Spending - Paying for Stuff

Sometimes when we pay for something, little is thought about the sources of the money used to make purchases. The sources of the money for purchases are present earnings, savings, charge accounts and loans. The cost of the purchase often determines the source. The "stuff" talked about in this chapter pertains to purchases not paid for by loans or mortgages. Later, Chapter V will discuss major purchases involving loans and mortgages.

Most often we pay for "stuff" from present earnings. For example, most people will pay for groceries from present earnings; however, a purchase of a refrigerator might be paid for from savings or a charge account. Purchases from present earnings should be considered first; however, since some purchases often exceed what can be paid for from present earnings, purchasing from savings or charge accounts must also be considered. Purchases made from savings preserve and do not obligate money from present and future earnings. Purchases from charge accounts erode and obligate present and future earnings. When purchases paid for from charge accounts are not paid in full within the billing cycle, finance charges will be incurred, and the cost of those purchases will increase debt. The bottom line is to think about the source of money when paying for stuff.

Purchases Using Present Earnings

Budgeting is critical for purchases from present earnings. Creating a budget can control tendencies to live above one's means. The discussion of purchasing from present earnings is like the discussion of spending from present earnings in Chapter I. Expenses are described as "fixed expenses" (rent, mortgage, car loan) and "variable expenses" (groceries, gas, dining out). Purchasing from present earnings is usually spending money for variable expenses.

The more you control what is purchased from present earnings, the more you control your future financial freedom and independence. If you have no savings and spend more than you earn, you charge for your purchases and will likely incur growing financial debt. Purchases paid for from present earnings should be "one and done" and not obligate future paychecks to pay for these purchases.

Purchases paid for from present earnings are perishable like food or short-lived items like dining out. When purchases are paid for with a credit card and the bill for the purchase is paid within the credit card billing cycle, that purchase is considered made from present earnings. Paying credit card bills in full is the goal but may not always be easy. It is an achievable goal with discipline.

Purchases Using Savings

Today, purchases paid for from savings seem to be an ancient concept. I was taught if you received money for a gift, set aside part of it to have available to buy something that may cost more than what you presently have. If you earned an allowance, I was taught to set aside part of it to save up for something that may cost more than your allowance. This was training and putting one in the mind-set that more expensive things can be purchased even when there is not enough money to buy that item in the present. Also, in the past for a variety of reasons, credit cards and loans were not always available to certain groups of people. Saving up for expensive purchases was the only way of enjoying finer things when money from present earnings was not enough.

Building and maintaining a savings are critical actions in developing a successful financial strategy to become a savvy consumer. Again, purchases paid for from savings preserve money available from current and future earnings. As discussed in Chapter II, savings can be created by allotments (allocation of salary to a savings account) or by "pay me first" (depositing a paycheck to savings and transferring money to checking to pay expenses). Also, savings can be created by making savings an expense item in a budget.

Today, parents should introduce the concept of saving to their children. Reaching for that easy assessable credit card to pay for things is a trap leading to mounting debt. However, when used properly, credit cards are a convenience and beneficial.

Purchases Using Charge Accounts

Purchases from charge accounts obligate present and future earnings. When charge accounts are used for purchasing variable expense items, often after a short while, we don't remember what the item was purchased. Charge account payments for perishable items can be stretched out for months. Paying for purchases over time in almost every instance will result in paying finance charges making the initial purchase cost more at the end. Purchasing over time with a credit card gives instant gratification; however, payments for that purchase will lessen future pay checks.

When Is Charging a Purchase Acceptable?

Charging is acceptable when the purchase is necessary and there is no other way to make the purchase. That purchase might be expensive and may necessitate a loan. As discussed in Chapter 1, this purchase can become a fixed expense. The purchase of a house or a car is not usually "one and done." These purchases are made one time but paid for monthly. The purchase becomes a reoccurring expense, fixed each month in the amount and payment date which should be included in your budget. The purchaser should remember that the longer the repayment term, the more the purchase costs because of finance charges.

Charging a purchase is also acceptable when those charges are paid in full before the end of the billing cycle to prevent finance charges. This practice briefly extends the payment of the purchase but is still considered a purchase from current earnings.

The Convenience of Credit Cards and Paying Bills with Credit Cards

There is no question that credit cards offer the convenience of not needing to carry a lot of cash and not needing to write checks. Also, payments with a credit card offer the convenience of a short-term loan. You can also track your spending (a tool for budgeting) and sometimes receive cash-back rewards and travel credits. But what about paying your bills with a credit card? Creditors love for customers to use autopay from a credit card. Signing up for auto-pay means authorizing a charge on a credit card on a particular day each month for a bill like a cell phone or utility bill. That offers bills to be paid and to be paid on time. Also, there is a savings of time in writing and mailing bills and a savings of expense in purchasing stamps. However, the convenience and the rewards can be off-set or lost when the credit card used to pay bills is not paid in full in the billing cycle to avoid finance charges. You must also be aware of certain companies will charge a convenience fee for paying with a credit card. Most often, without a plan, using credit cards to pay bills leads to growing debt and financial chaos.

Incentive Purchases - Interest Free/No Payment Purchases – A Trojan Horse (Don't Believe the Hype)

Often associated with holiday specials or promotions, an interest free purchase is an "incentive" purchase that can be made without incurring finance charges on the unpaid balance for a certain period. A no payment purchase is an "incentive" purchase where the full cost of the purchase is charged to your account, but monthly payments might not start for a certain period. Sounds good but credit card companies would not offer these "incentives" unless they could make money from them. These incentives are offered sometimes in stores to get people to sign-up for the stores' credit card. These offers often have high interest rates with them and you must read the fine print. These credit card companies know that a certain number of folks will not follow the rules in fine print and at the end of the promotional or grace period, the companies have to the right to charge finance charges that were once exempt during the promotion and those finance charges may be even higher than those during regular times. Many times, in these promotions, a purchase is made and the detailed paperwork is given to the customer; however, no monthly statements are sent. The customer soon forgets that the terms of the purchase which may state that unless a payment is made before the expiration of the promotional period, all finance charges will be enforced.

The bottom line to how you "Pay for Stuff" is limiting the amount of credit card purchases unless the credit card purchases are paid in full within a billing cycle. The goal is to preserve present and future earnings. There are financial rewards in following this plan, but it requires discipline and a plan. Falling into the trap of mounting debt can be avoided and a financial stable, even a modest luxury lifestyle can be obtained by understanding how to preserve and protect present and future earnings by minimizing paying for "stuff" over time.

Paying for College – Student Loans

Student loans – a blessing or a curse! Student loans are a blessing when they are the only means of going to college. Student loans are a curse when they are misused and abused.

Student Loans – A Blessing

When the only way to pay for college is a student loan, student loans are a blessing; however, study is needed to determine how much of a loan is appropriate and whether your college choice is affordable. Nerdwallet suggests that student loan payments be no greater than 10% of take-home pay. For example, if you research salaries by occupation and the starting salary for your college major is $50,000, the amount of a student loan you can afford to borrow is $27,909.24

based on a 10-year loan, a 3.75% interest rate, and a $2792.00 per month take-home pay. Nerdwallet's student loan affordability calculator can be a tool to use to make a reason decision about a student loan.

Student Loans – A Curse

It is quite simple; student loans obligate future earnings and limit future borrowing power by increasing debt-to-income ratio. College students enter the workforce with their future paychecks obligated to their student loans. In 2021, Student Loan Debt reached $1.7 trillion and U.S. borrowers with Student Loan Debt were 45 million. Sadly, borrowers ages 50 – 61 owed $262.2 billion (6.2 million borrowers) and borrowers age 62 and over owed $86.8 billion (2.3 million borrowers). For some, that is nearly lifetime of being in student loan debt. In 2017, the average interest rate across all student loans was 5.8%. In 2021, the average student loan debt was $37,693 with a 11.1 delinquency rate and $122.2 billion (5.5 million borrowers) in cumulative default. For many, these statistics strongly suggest student loans are a curse.

There are other ways to attend college without going into debt. Applying for a scholarship or a grant is one. In either case, the money does not have to be repaid. Setting up a college fund is another way to avoid going into debt. Family, friends and others can contribute to a fund for your college education. Working your way through school is another way of satisfying your financial needs. Federal work-study programs and university jobs are sometimes available. While these options may not completely cover all expenses, they may reduce the amount of debt that would be associated with a student loan.

Chapter IV.

Setting Aside Money

Sometimes the hardest thing to do is to set aside money; however, it could be the most important thing to do to achieve financial independence and success. It is the foundation of living like a millionaire but not being a millionaire. While in general, money set aside will be in a savings account, that savings account can be separated into three categories – Emergency Funds, Rainy Day Funds and Savings Accounts.

Emergency Funds

What is an "emergency fund?" An emergency fund is money set aside for expenses associated with a job loss, major illness, or other unexpected catastrophic financial occurrences. In the event of a job loss, an emergency fund should be large enough to cover 3 – 6 months of living expenses. An emergency fund should be liquid like a savings account which could be accessed quickly in a financial emergency. If used, it should be as quickly as possible replenished.

Rainy-Day Funds

A "rainy day" fund is money set aside for expenses associated with unplanned financial occurrences like an appliance breakdown, car breakdown or a repair that is expected but the timing is unknown. Rainy day funds are for less severe events causing expenses while emergency funds are for catastrophic events. The size of a rainy-day fund could be as much as 1/3 or 1/4 of an emergency fund. Also, the size could be tied to the cost, age and condition of your car and appliances. Replenishing a rainy-day fund is also dependent on circumstances or conditions of daily used items, such as your car or appliances.

Savings Accounts

Savings accounts are for <u>planned</u> events like saving up for a new computer. Savings accounts are created for specific amounts and for a specific time period. Saving accounts can be used to build wealth. Savings accounts differ from emergency funds and rainy-day fund because savings accounts are for known events while emergency and rainy-day funds are for unplanned and unexpected events. Chapter II discusses savings accounts in more detail. When thinking about the three categories of Set Aside Money, keep this table in mind:

Set Aside Money		
Category	Purpose	Example
Emergency Funds	Unexpected catastrophic events	Job loss, major illness
Rainy-Day Funds	Unplanned events	Appliance or car breakdown
Savings Accounts	Planned events	Saving for a new computer

Money Set Aside in One Account? No!

While it is certainly true that emergency and rainy-day funds can be put into a savings account, it is better to keep emergency funds, rainy day funds and savings separate to stay away from one fund accidently taking money away from another fund. Separate categories establish boundaries and certainty when events planned or unplanned occur.

Keeping separate accounts may take more work but it will have the advantage of offering more monthly withdrawals. For emergency funds, rainy day funds and savings accounts, banks and financial institutions may allow only 6 withdrawals per month per account without penalty or fee. If emergency funds, rainy day funds and savings are in separate accounts, more withdrawals will be available in an emergency or for other reasons.

Chapter V.

Purchasing

When making a purchase, an unwritten rule should be that you know how long it will take to pay for the purchase. For minor purchases, not much thought is necessary since those purchases can be made from current earnings and be a "one and done" transaction. However, for major purchases, purchases not made from current earnings, before a sale is final, you should know how long it will take to pay for that purchase. Understanding how to make purchases can be a key to financial success, independence and living large.

The Relationship between Purchases and Expense

When a purchase is made, an expense results. That expense can be one-and-done by paying cash or writing a check. That expense can be paid for over time by charging or taking out a loan. A minor purchase is related to variable expense. A major purchase is related to fixed expense. This table shows it all:

Example	Purchase Type	Expense Type	Reason
Car	Major	Fixed	Fixed payments on a specific schedule
Groceries	Minor	Variable	Variable payment on a sometime variable schedule
House	Major	Fixed	Fixed payments on a specific schedule
Gas (Auto)	Minor	Variable	Variable payment on a sometime variable schedule
Dining out	Minor	Variable	Variable payment on a sometime variable schedule

Minor Purchases

In general, a minor purchase is a purchase that can be made from current earnings. Since earnings vary over time, what one might consider a minor purchase today can be something different tomorrow. As discussed in Chapter III, "Paying for Stuff," expenses paid for from current earnings are usually "variable" expenses (gas, groceries, dining out). "Fixed" expenses are rent, car note, mortgage, things that are paid the same amount on a specific day each month. Therefore, minor purchases are also variable expenses, like a trip to McDonalds, things that are not paid in the same amount and not paid on the same day of the month. Minor purchases are usually inexpensive and can be short-lived, for example the purchase of a ticket to the movies or a concert. Minor purchases can also be one-and-done purchases, such as a visit to the barber or the hairdresser. The event may happen again, but the purchase is done only once. Minor purchases should not be paid for over time, in other words, charged, unless the purchase is paid in full before finance charges accrue on the credit card used for the purchase.

Major Purchases

A major purchase is usually a purchase that cannot be paid for from current earnings. In general, a major purchase is paid for from (1) savings or over time either from (2) a charge account or (3) a loan. The cost of a major purchase can determine which of these three options will be chosen. Savings is money set aside and Chapter IV, "Money Set Aside" talks about three options for paying for purchases which cannot be paid for from current earnings. The three options related to paying from money set aside are emergency funds, rainy day funds and savings accounts. See Chapter IV for that discussion.

Major Purchases Paid for Over Time

A major purchase paid for over time is a purchase paid for from either a charge account or a loan. Again, the cost of a major purchase will determine which of these two options will be chosen. Replacing your refrigerator or hot water heater is considered a major purchase; however, compared to purchasing a car or a house, they cost considerably less. Therefore, purchasing a refrigerator or hot water heater might be paid for from money set aside or paid for over time while purchasing a car or a house will likely almost always be paid for over time. As mention earlier, before the sale is final, you should know how long it will take to pay for the purchase. If you know how long it will take to pay for a purchase, you can then avoid a purchase becoming an unending debt. A plan can be developed as part of your budget that will identify the end of debt.

Charge Accounts

A charge account is a revolving account secured by a credit card. It is called a revolving account because it is an account with a financial institution that allows a customer to pay in full to a vendor and charge it to an account on which the customer pays periodically or monthly something less than the full cost of the purchase until the balance is paid in full. The unpaid balance is carried or "revolved" each month until the cost of the purchase is paid in full. The financial institution adds a fee (interest/finance charge/carrying charge) to the balance for allowing the customer to purchase an item that the customer could not pay for from current earnings or set aside money.

It is not likely that a car or a house will be paid for from a charge account. While an appliance might be paid for from current earnings if you are paid above average wages, it will likely be paid for from a charge account. Please see Chapter III, Section C - "Purchases Paid for from Charge Account" for further discussion and warnings about incentive purchases.

Loans

For most people, the largest purchases leading to the most significant loans are cars and homes. Other large purchases are boats and recreational vehicles which some will buy; however, a house for most will be the largest purchase that will ever be made. The discussion below is an introduction to some of the things to consider when making a purchase of a car or a home. Further study should be done.

Cars

Buying a car whether new or used is an exciting time. Searching for the right color and right model with the features you want can be fun. When looking for a car, researching on Cars.com, Cargurus.com, Edmunds.com and others offer valuable information in choosing the right vehicle. While many will purchase a car over time and experience a car note, it is Important to understanding that buying gas, maintenance, insurance and repairs are a few expenses of car ownership that are in addition to a car note. A wise first step is to look at your budget to determine how much you can afford for a car. From the basic example in Chapter I, take home pay is $2500.00 per month and only four expenses are listed. That is far fewer than what most people will have in expenses. If all additional expenses (including savings) other than car expenses are listed and they amount to $2000.00 per month, then $500.00 per month is left for owning a car. However, it is important to know that $500.00 per month is **not** what should be paid in a car note for owning a car. The true cost of car ownership includes the expense of a car note, gas, maintenance, repairs and insurance for a start. While focus in this book is on car note, the total cost of car ownership is noted to be about twice the cost of a car note in a survey by the Bureau of Statistics Consumer Expenditures Survey in 2017. If you are purchasing your first car and have no idea of the additional cost of car ownership, estimating that the additional expenses of car ownership may be as much as a car note may be a good number to put in your budget.

In the third quarter of 2018, the credit reporting bureau Experian reported that 85% of new car buyers and 53% of used car buyers took out an auto loan to purchase their cars. You have more control of the loan process that you may realize. Once you decided on the car you want, shop for financing before going to a dealership. Most institutions offering car loans will have a monthly note calculator, so you can add something for taxes, title and dealer costs to compute a monthly car note. This monthly car note will not likely be exact, but it will give you an idea of what to expect. Keep in mind the total cost of car ownership and adjust the terms in the calculator to get a monthly note that will work in your budget. If that figure is not achieved, then choose another car that will work in your budget.

The exercise above determines a price range for the car you can afford. Now try to be preapproved from your bank, credit union or any institution offering car loans. **Look for the shortest term and lowest interest rate** and don't forget about online lenders. Remember that a longer-term loan, may mean you can purchase a more expensive car; however, you will pay more interest and it is possible that the value of your car will go down faster than the unpaid balance of your loan. That means if you are in an accident and your car needs to be replaced, you may owe more on your car than the insurance company is willing to pay to replace your car. It also means that if you are trading in your car before paying it off, your trade in value might be less than what you owe on your car. With preapproved financing, you can compare the financing offered by a dealer. Choose what works best for you.

No Money Down

No money down means financing the total cost of the car, taxes, title and dealer costs. It sounds good, but this financing comes sometimes with longer term loans and higher interest rates. Also, unless the cost of the car that you are purchasing is significantly below the retail value of the car, purchasing a car with no down payment can lead to a later value of the car that is less than the loan balance. Having a down payment lowers the loan amount and sometimes results in more favorable terms and interest rates.

Trade-ins

You must know the value of your car if you plan to trade it in for another vehicle. Also, if you have a loan on your trade-in, you must know its value with respect to how much you owe on it. Again, research on Cars.com, Cargurus.com, Edmunds.com and others can used to determine the value of your car. Now, when you go to the dealer, you will know if the dealer is giving you a fair value on your trade-in. Your trade-in can serve as a down payment on your next vehicle. It will bring down the cost that you will be financing and create a lower monthly payment.

Upside-down in a Loan

Upside-down is negative equity. You are upside-down in a loan when the value of your car or home is less than what you owe on your loan. This may happen when your previous car loan was at a long term or a high interest rate which meant that your loan balance was going down at a slower rate than the rate at which your car lost value. For example, you are upside-down in a loan when your car's value is $1000.00 and your loan on that car is $1500.00. If you are looking for another car, a dealer may say "no problem" and you can still buy that car you want despite being upside-down. The dealer will then include the amount you owe on your trade-in into your new loan. **Bad idea.** This deal means you will be paying for your old car and new car at the same time for the duration of the new loan. Once you add more to the cost of the loan on your new car, you create another opportunity to be upside-down on your new car. Therefore, in the next 4 or 5 years when you look to trade-in the car you are now purchasing, you might end up with a note carrying the cost of 2 cars you no longer own. It becomes a generational curse.

Homes

A home is where you go when you leave work, where your kids go when they leave school and where you feel safe when you close your eyes at night. A home is the largest purchase that most of us will make in our lifetime. It is something that should not be rushed. Giving proper detail and study to purchase a home is mandatory and it could take 6 months or much longer. This text will not attempt to discuss the many aspects of shopping for a home, but touch on only things to consider when obtaining a loan (mortgage).

Mortgage

A mortgage is a loan agreement between a lender and you that allows you to purchase over time a home that the lender can take if you fail to repay the money you owe. Because of the high cost of homes, the purchaser requires a long-term loan of 15, 20, 25 or 30 years. That loan is secured by the home being bought (collateral).

Just like purchasing a car, the first step in purchasing a home is determining how much house you can afford. That means looking back at your budget. Looking at your income and expenses excluding living expenses like current rent and associated expenses can be the first estimate of how much house you can afford. The budget for the house you can afford must include not only your mortgage which may include property taxes, homeowners' insurance, homeowners' association dues but also utility expense and upkeep expense. Lenders on the internet have various tools to help in estimating how much house you can afford. A tool called a "home affordability calculator" is available at Zillow.com.

Pre-approval

Shop for your mortgage and get pre-approved. Getting pre-approved is getting an independent assessment of your financial health and your ability to pay for a house. A pre-approved loan shows the maximum amount that a lender is willing to loan you to purchase a house. That does not mean you need to purchase a house costing that much. The monthly payment on your pre-approved loan should resemble what you determined to be what you can budget without utilities. If your budget amount for a mortgage is greater than the monthly payment in your pre-approved loan, you have probably overestimated what you can afford of a house. If your budget amount for a mortgage is less that the monthly payment in your pre-approved loan, that is good because your financial situation is probably better than you thought, and you will probably be better able to handle home ownership.

Part of shopping for a mortgage is your credit score. When purchasing a home, your credit score can determine your ability to obtain a loan and obtain a loan at a lower interest rate. A loan at a lower interest rate means paying a lower monthly payment for the loan or having the ability to buy a more expensive house at a given monthly payment. At the start of looking for a mortgage, prospective home buyers should get their credit reports which are available free at least once a year from the three major credit reporting agencies, TransUnion, Equifax and Experian. Among other things, a 720 or higher credit score could result in not only obtaining a mortgage, but also a favorable interest rate on a loan. The bottom line is to know your credit score which if you can improve it, may enable you to obtain a better loan.

Down Payments

Unless you are in the military, a veteran or a rural or suburban buyer in some instances, you will need a down payment to obtain a loan to purchase a house. According to Nerdwallet, for a conventional loan (loans not guaranteed by the federal government), at least a 3% down payment is required. For an FHA loan (loans backed by the Federal Housing Administration), a minimum 3.5% down payment is needed. Traditional banks and lending institutions like borrowers to have a 20% down payment to obtain a loan. When borrowers do not have a 20% down payment and have at least the minimum down payment, they can still obtain a loan which now includes PMI (Private Mortgage Insurance). PMI is an insurance that protects the lender when you do not have at least a 20% down payment. Because the lender accepts additional risks for loans with down payments less than 20%, the lender will include PMI in the monthly mortgage that the buyer pays. According to Chase Bank, PMI can be between .22% to 2.25% of the original loan amount. Based on that, PMI for a $400,000 loan would cost $73.33 to $750.00 per month. The cost of

PMI depends on many things including the size of the mortgage, the down payment, your credit score and the type of mortgage (fixed-rate or adjustable rate). A fixed rate mortgage has the same interest rate over the life of the loan and is sometimes higher than the initial interest rate on an adjustable-rate loan. An adjustable-rate mortgage (ARM) has an adjustable interest rate which can increase and sometimes can become more expensive over the life of a loan.

Down Payment Woes

For many, even a 3.5% down payment for a home purchase is just not possible. Fortunately, there are options. If your family is wealthy, FHA will allow borrowers to use gift money to pay a down payment. Throughout the United States, there are First-Time Home Buyer Grants and Loans Programs. Research is necessary to determine which program is best for you. Sellers got involved with this issue by absorbing the down payment for buyers by raising the selling price. Mortgage debt increased beyond what many could afford. This and other practices led to housing crises of 2008 and the creation of the Housing and Economic Recovery Act of 2008 which prohibited such programs.

There are many innovative ways of receiving down payer assistance and it is up to the borrower to research the many private and government programs. It is important to understand that assistance will sometimes come with a cost and understanding whether that cost exceeds your budget is paramount.

The Importance of Having Equity

Sometime having a down payment is not possible; however, when possible, having a down payment is beneficial. Down payments on large purchases creates equity in the purchase and allows sometimes more favorable terms for loans. For the purchase of a car, having a down payment can mean not being upside down in a loan or having negative equity. Cars depreciate or lose value the minute you purchase them. Making a down payment puts you in a more favorable position at the end of ownership since the balance owed if any, will be less and your trade-in value and money for replacement after a total loss accident will be more. The disadvantages of negative equity in car ownership have been discussed on page 38 under "Upside-down in a loan."

For the purchase of a home, having a down payment creates equity and allows for more favorable loan terms. As mentioned already, when your mortgage is less than 80% of the value of your home, you can avoid the extra expense of PMI. Also, having equity in your home allows you to be your banker. With equity in your home, you may be able to open a home equity loan or a home equity line of credit (HELOC). Only responsible financially able persons should consider using the equity in their homes because their homes become collateral securing their loans. A home equity loan and a HELOC are second mortgages. A home equity loan is usually a loan for a fixed amount, a fixed term and sometimes a fixed interest rate. A HELOC is a loan where the lender establishes a maximum loan amount for a period and the borrower has a draw on money up to the maximum loan amount and can pay down the loan until the term ends and the balance owed is due. The advantage of a HELOC is that the borrowed money can be used for just about anything, but it should be used prudently and not be used for every-day expenses. Usually, the interest on these loans is deductible under Federal and State tax laws; however, since 2017, interest on HELOCs is not deductible unless the loan is used for a substantial home improvement. According to many lenders in 2021, because of market uncertainties stemming from the COVID-19 pandemic, HELOCs have been put on pause.

Be Your Own Loan Officer

Sometimes we rely on others to tell us if we can afford a purchase when we know our financial details. If we have a budget and know our credit worthiness, the first person to approve your application for a purchase should be you. If you have been diligent in your financial affairs and you know the cost of a purchase, you know already if you can afford it. Find out your credit score, know your debt-to-income ratio, ask yourself if you would loan you money based on your financial details. If you are in a strong position, go after loans with the best terms. Since lenders make money from you, be selective and make the lender earn your business. Be realistic and confident that you have prepared and positioned yourself to approve yourself for a loan and go for it, full steam ahead to find the best loan for your purchase.

Know How Long It Will Take to Pay for Purchases

Why is it important to know how long it will take to pay for purchases? It is important to know because not knowing will cost you time and money. A simple example is when minor purchases accumulate to become major purchases. As purchases accumulate and unpaid balances grow, the length of payment and the amount of interest increases. An example is a credit card brand new with a $1000.00 limit. You use it for everyday purchases but never pay the balance owed on the card in full when the bill comes.

Case Study

Adrian plans to attend her friend's wedding two months away. She plans to purchase shoes, dress, purse, stockings, perfume, underclothes and jewelry a month before the event. Like most people, Adrian has not thought about how long it will take to pay for those purchases. The bottom line in this example is that if she charges all of her purchases, it will take Adrian almost two years and $104.00 in interest expense to pay for her purchases. On the other hand, if Adrian thinks about paying cash for the less expensive items of shoes, stockings, perfume and underclothing and for the things she charged, paying above the minimum payment on her bill, she will pay for in full the more expensive dress, purse and jewelry in 8 months and pay only $25.92 in interest. Please observe the chart below:

| | | Credit Card | | Payment | | | |
Date	Merchandise	Charges	Balance	Minimum Monthly	Months to Reach Full Payment	Total	Interest Payments
		Charging everything for the wedding					
Day 1	shoes	$60.00	$60.00				
Day 8	dress	$125.00	$185.00				
Day 10	purse	$125.00	$310.00				
Day 12	stocking	$8.00	$318.00				
Day 14	perfume	$50.00	$368.00				
Day 18	underclothes	$30.00	$398.00				
Day 25	jewelry	$104.00	$502.00				
Bill from Credit Card Company at End of the Month				$27.00	23 months	$606.00	$104.00

Date	Merchandise	Charges	Balance	Your Choice of Payment	Months to Reach Full Payment	Total Payments	Interest Payments
		Paying cash for shoes, stockings, perfume and underclothes					
Day 1	shoes						
Day 8	dress	$125.00	$125.00				
Day 10	purse	$125.00	$250.00				
Day 12	stocking						
Day 14	perfume						
Day 18	underclothes						
Day 25	jewelry	$104.00	$354.00				
Bill from Credit Card Company at End of the Month				$50.00	8 months	$379.92	$25.92

15 months savings in payments and $78.08 in interest by paying cash for minor items

Timing of Major Purchases

Timing of major purchases should reflect planning of anticipated events. Major appliances and cars do not last forever. If you know that your washer and dryer are eight years old, start planning for replacements. Your car is ten years old and repairs are becoming more frequent. Start planning for another car before the transmission fails. While this discussion sounds a lot like the discussion "Rainy-day Funds" in Chapter IV, Setting Aside Money," it is different. Rainy-day Funds are for unplanned repairs and Timing of Major Purchases concerns replacement of major items.

Major Purchases before Retirement

As you approach retirement If you have been in your house twenty years and never replaced your refrigerator, hot water heater or roof, plan to replace those items before you retire. Most likely, your income will be less in retirement, so set up a fund to get those major purchases out of the way before you retire. If it is within your budget and you considered remodeling or an addition to the house you plan to have in retirement, do this also before you retire. Taking as few big-ticket purchases into retirement as possible will increase your comfort in your senior years.

Purchase with Cash or by Financing

Chapter IV discussed setting aside money in emergency funds, rainy-day funds and savings account. Some will successfully set aside money above the amount needed for emergency and rainy-day funds, to the extent of being able to purchase from savings a major item like a car which for most people will be financed. The question then becomes should one pay cash from savings or finance a major purchase like a car. The obvious reason for paying cash is the elimination of finance charges; but when the interest rate for financing is less than the interest rate on savings, financing may be appropriate. Conversely, if the interest rate for financing is greater than the interest rate on savings, purchasing from savings may be appropriate.

For example, you have set aside money in an online-savings-account paying .5%. You plan to buy a car that would result in a $25,000 loan for 5 years at a 3% interest rate and a car note of $449.22 per month. If you finance your car, you will pay $1,953.20 in interest over 5 years. If you leave $25,000 in the bank for 5 years you will earn $632.74. **By paying cash, you will forego the interest earned to save $1,320.46 in interest expense ($1,953.20 - $632.74).** Another thought is if you decide to deposit the car note that you would pay if financing, after 5 years, your savings account will equal $27,298.55 based on monthly deposits of $449.22 plus interest earned. **In other words, by paying cash for your car and depositing a fake car note in the bank, you will end up with $2,298.55 more than the $25,000 removed from the bank to pay for the car.**

Financing your car makes sense when you can earn more by leaving your money in the bank or with the services of a financial advisor investing your money to earn more than the expense you would be paying for financing your purchase. In the previous example, a savings account or investment with more than 1.51% return after any fees would generate more in interest than the $1,953.20 in finance charges associated with a car loan. The above example is basic and did not consider inflation or any other factor that could affect the time-value of money.

Financial Advisor

While we may know how to save, we may not know how to invest. We need to invest to maximize the return on our money. If in the previous example, we did not need to purchase a car, the money available to buy a car would need to be invested rather than to remain in a low interest rate savings account. The concern with investing is that money you start with is not always guaranteed to be returned to you. Speaking with a financial advisor who is trustworthy will enable you to develop an investment strategy based on your age, risk tolerance and investment goals. Since that person will be working for you, be selective and explore the field to choose someone you can trust and be confident that your interest comes first. Understand the cost of having a financial advisor and prepare a cost/benefit analysis of the service. Take the time necessary to choose someone who will be there for the long-term.

Chapter VI.

Being in Credit Card Debt

Mismanaging Credit Card Debt

Today, credit cards are a necessary convenience. The problem is that we charge our cards, and many times forget what we charge on them. That is what credit card companies want and count on. How many of us charge something and then write a note to remind ourselves of what was just charged. For example, at the beginning of the month, you have an open account at Macy's with a balance from the previous month of $1415.00 and a minimum payment of $45.00 due. But you used that card 5 times during the month for a shirt, $35.00; shoes, $65.00; gas, $35.00 and two other charges for $40.00 each that you can't remember. You say you will be smart and pay twice the minimum payment or $90.00. And the credit card company laughs because your debt is growing.

- Balance start of the month = $1415.00
- 29% interest on the previous month's balance = $34.20
- Charges during the month = $215.00
- Payment = $90.00
- Balance after bill is paid = $1574.20, ($1415.00 + $34.20 +$215.00 - $90.00 = $1574.20)
- Increase in balance at end of the month = $159.20

Now the next month is somebody's birthday or it's Christmas. The balance grows again and the credit card company generously gave you a $5,000.00 limit on your card. The next thing you know that card is maxed and your car needs tires. At your expense, the party has just started.

Eliminating Debt

Many of us have money to pay our bills but believe that paying on time and paying a little more than the amount due, while still using those credit cards, is responsible behavior. NO! NO! NO! Practicing this behavior over the last 10 years, Tanya has run up a credit card debt of $57,794.00 on eleven credit cards. Tanya consistently pays $1787.00 monthly to the credit card companies. She pays a little more than the minimum payment due monthly on each of the cards while continuing to use the cards that are not maxed out. With this strategy she will never get out of debt. The credit card companies tell us this in the payment information of our bills. Tanya's Macy's bill in the previous paragraph clearly states that (a) it takes 8 years to pay her balance provided she makes no more purchases on her card and she pays the minimum bill and (b) again making no new purchases, it takes 3 years to pay her balance paying $5 over the minimum payment. Macy's explains this on every bill sent.

There is "The Plan" to eliminate all of Tanya's credit card debt in less than 5 years. The plan is simple. It is to **apply the overpayment of all bills to the bill with the lowest balance while at the same time, continue to pay the minimum payment on all of the other bills.** "The Plan" is for someone who is good at paying bills but maybe not good at managing debt.

The first six columns of "The Plan" in the table below are based on current information coming from current credit card information and current payment practices. The last three columns are based on implementing "The Plan." Don't be intimidated by the numbers. Take time to study "The Plan."

"THE PLAN"

Credit Card	6/1/2020 Balance	Minimum Payment	June 2020 Actual Payment	June over Payment	No. of Months to Pay Balance at Min Payment	Per plan	"The Plan" Final Payment	Reward Money
A	$1,392.99	$45.00	$50.00	$5.00	49	8	2/22/2021	$94.72
B	$1,818.00	$41.00	$50.00	$9.00	120	14	8/10/2021	$209.30
C	$2,088.00	$72.00	$75.00	$3.00	46	17	11/10/2021	$22.39
D	$3,421.00	$95.00	$145.00	$50.00	72	24	6/10/2022	$19.88
E	$3,734.00	$95.00	$110.00	$15.00	84	30	12/10/2022	$29.03
F	$4,582.00	$140.00	$157.00	$17.00	58	34	4/10/2023	$222.37
G	$4,906.00	$161.00	$165.00	$4.00	49	36	6/10/2023	$175.91
H	$6,781.00	$162.00	$175.00	$13.00	97	42	12/10/2023	$596.65
I	$7,344.00	$169.00	$180.00	$11.00	109	47	5/10/2024	$1,126.65
J	$10,380.00	$316.00	$330.00	$14.00	58	48	6/10/2024	$1,196.65
K	$11,326.00	$334.00	$350.00	$16.00	59	49	7/10/2024	$1,316.24
		$1,630.00	$1,787.00	$157.00				$5,009.78

How does this work?

The above example is based on Tanya's payment habits which involved paying a little more than her minimum balance on each of her cards. **First** you list your bills lowest to highest, including finance rate, minimum payment and number of months to pay the balance. Based on this list, put the list in order of the easiest to the hardest bills to eliminate. Most likely, you will list your bills according to lowest to highest balances. Ideally, credit card balances monthly should be paid in full in order to avoid finance charges; however, when balances have gotten out of hand, this plan is designed to get out of debt and develop financial stability.

Second, add the June over-payment of the bills which sum to $157.00. **Third**, add the June over-payment total to the minimum payment for the easiest bill to eliminate, Credit Card A, to get the total monthly payment for Credit Card A. The numbers are $157.00 + $45.00 = $202.00.

The payments for July 2020 are $202.00 for Credit Card A and the minimum payment for all other credit cards. Appendix A contains the payment schedule for each credit card based on following "The Plan."

Reward Money

Plans are hard to stick to, so the Reward Money is a reward for sticking to "The Plan" and is awarded in the month of the final payment for each credit card. It is the difference in scheduled payment and the balance owed on each card's final payment. Appendix B shows the final schedule payment for Credit Card is $202.00 and the balance owed for the final payment is $107.28; therefore the Reward Money is $202.00 - $107.28 = $94.72. While the Reward Money varies for each credit card, over the life of the plan, the total Reward Money equals $5,009.78. Appendix B contains details for all credit cards in "The Plan" for Tanya.

Chapter VII.

Retirement

Retirement is and should be a permanent departure from the workforce. It is the stoppage of required day-to-day activity necessary to earn wages. Retirement can be voluntary or involuntary. If retirement is voluntary, it can be planned. If it is involuntary, it usually is unexpected and may be due to disability. This chapter discusses voluntary retirement which in the United States has been for many at age 65.

When Can I Retire?

The direct answer to this question is you can retire when you are prepared to retire. Being prepared to retire means prepared financially, physically and mentally.

Financially Prepared for Retirement

Being financially ready for retirement can start the first day of your first job. It is setting a budget that includes a plan for retirement. That plan can be one offered by your employer or one that you develop or better still, a plan for retirement that includes both your employer's plan and your independent plan. This chapter is last because the preceding chapters prepare one financially for retirement. If you have budgeted (Chapter I), saved (Chapter II), paid for stuff prudently (Chapter III), compartmentalize savings (Chapter IV), navigated minor and major purchases (Chapter V) and managed debt (Chapter VI), you are financially ready for retirement.

Physically Prepared for Retirement

Preparing physically for retirement means having a plan for physical activities for the hours that you were required to be at work before retirement. These activities can be exercising, gathering socially, traveling, working a part time job and doing the other things that you may now have time to do. Having no plans, idle time and aimless wandering will not contribute to a long rewarding retirement. Physical preparation for retirement means also keeping on top of your physical health and having regular checkups.

Mentally Prepared for Retirement

Retirement is a life change and mental preparation for it should start years before actual retirement. Time off without a planned vacation should reveal what it feels like to get up and not go to work. Are you bored or do you plan your day? If you were going to work, you might get up at 6:00 am, so will you still get up that early or get up when you feel like it? To prepare mentally for retirement examine your mental needs for peace and harmony. If you feel blessed to have been able to retire, consider volunteering to bless others. Take charge of your life and free your spirit to make retirement a rewarding and exciting new chapter of your life. Mental needs are not the same for everyone, so develop a plan for retirement that is mentally for you.

Living Large

The title of this book, "I don't want to be a millionaire; I just want to live like one" is about living large for anyone who is disciplined and wise. Living large implies being wealthy; but being disciplined and wise can make up for not being rich. Being disciplined, wise and setting achievable goals can be the foundation of a plan for successful financial independence and living large. "Wisdom and money can get you almost anything, but only wisdom can save your life."

Ecclesiastes 7:12, New Living Translation. The chapters in this book lay out a plan and are summarized next:

Budgeting

In Chapter I, three phases of earnings and spending were discussed. Having goals when you enter the workforce (Phase 1), when you enter midcareer employment (Phase 2) and when you enter retirement (Phase 3) are very important in developing a livable and doable budget.

Savings

Chapter II discusses allotments and "Pay me first" as a way of saving. With a budget featuring "pay me first," saving is easier and done without much thought.

Spending

While expenses can be fixed or variable, as discussed in Chapter III, "paying for stuff" is usually paying for variable expenses. Fixed expenses are rent, mortgages and car loans. Variable expenses are groceries, gas, dining out and more. Creating a plan for paying for variable expenses, "stuff," that minimizes credit card debt sets the basis for protecting future earnings and creates the opportunity for living large.

Setting Money Aside

Savings is setting money aside; however, as mentioned in Chapter IV it can be separated in three separate accounts to avoid subsidizing one account to the detriment of another account. The separated accounts are distinct in purpose, and they are an emergency account, a rainy-day account and a savings account. The emergency account's purpose is for job loss, major illness or another unexpected catastrophic financial calamity. The rainy-day account is for expenses associated with unplanned financial occurrences like an appliance breakdown, car breakdown or a repair that is expected but the timing is unknown. The purpose of the savings account is for planned activity for specific amounts and for a specific time. For example, you may plan to save for purchasing a new computer within the next six months. Maintaining three separate accounts for setting money aside goes beyond the normal requirements for savings; but the rewards are worth the effort.

Purchasing

As Chapter V discusses, understanding how to make purchases can be a key to financial success, independence and living large. Making minor purchases from current earnings is important. It means <u>not</u> allowing the unpaid balance of minor purchases to carry over or revolve to the balance owed on credit cards to the next month. It also means <u>not</u> allowing credit card debt to grow because of minor purchases.

Unless you are a high salaried person, major purchases are not paid from current earnings. Major purchases are paid for from savings or over time either from a charge account or a loan.   While understanding that major purchases cannot always be paid for from savings, understanding how to make a major purchase contributes to financial success, independence and living large. This means having equity in major purchases for which a loan has been secured. For an auto, it means the value of your car is greater than the amount you owe on it. When purchasing a home, it means you have at least 20% equity in the house you are purchasing to avoid additional expense for mortgage insurance which would be included in your loan payment and be substantial.

Debt

"Adult" and "in debt" sound a little alike; however, drowning in debt does not have to be part of adult life. Can an adult live large and be in debt? Yes, if debt is managed. Chapter VI explains managing debt and eliminating debt. Debt is managed by minimizing its growth. Sometimes, increasing debt is unavoidable, but having a plan to eliminate debt is possible. Chapter VI illustrates elimination of nearly $58 thousand of credit card debt in less than five years. Chapter VI, also, explains a plan for "Reward Money" for sticking to a plan to eliminate debt.

Retirement

Chapter VII asks, "when can I retire?" and it answers when you are prepared financially, physically and mentally. Chapter VII also talks about "living large" and summarizes the chapters in this book as a plan for achieving this goal.

AFTERWORD

How can you say that you don't want to be a millionaire; but just live like one? The author of this book has said this and has practiced what he preached. He shows that the backbone of not being a millionaire but living like one is "**BSS**" – **B**udgeting, **S**aving and **S**pending. Practicing "BSS," the author navigated through (Chapter 1) Just Entering the Workforce (Phase 1), Mid-Career Employment (Phase 2) and then Retirement (Phase 3). Just entering the workforce after college, the author and his bride could not qualify for an apartment renting for $100 a month. They lived for two years with the author's mother, started a family, budgeted and saved for their first house. With a mechanical engineering degree, the author climbed a career ladder while at the same time responsibilities increased. In addition to handling his family's finances, he managed the finances of his aging mother and the finances of a travel agency he owned with some business partners. As chairman of his church administrative council, he was asked to give up that position to become treasurer. Initially, he thought there was no way to add the responsibility of the church's finances which alone eclipsed the financial concerns of his three other responsibilities. Praying on it, he took a job which the past two treasures held for no more than 6 months each and he stayed in that position for nearly 6 years.

Unknown to him at that time, he established a covenant with God that allowed him to practice successfully "BSS" and not be a millionaire but live like one. Not to be taken as bragging, but a statement of fact, the author's possessions suggest "living large." Since entering the workforce to now living in retirement, the author has owned at one time three houses and at various times Mercedes and Porsches. Entering retirement living in a modest 1132 sq ft home, the author began a second career as a consultant for Brown, Williams, Moorehead and Quinn, Inc., energy consulting firm. Compared to his pre-retirement income, his income in retirement doubled. Despite this fortune, the author reduced his hours as a consultant and soon devoted his time to his travel business and volunteer work. Opposite of reducing expenses in retirement, the author purchased a new 4000 sq ft home when his income was shrinking. It became obvious that his covenant with God was enabling him to a lot with little. He was not being a millionaire but living like one.

While throughout his lifetime, the author was able to follow the plans and strategies in this text, the author recognizes that many will not, but he hopes that some will find useful some of the practices presented in his book.

APPENDIX A

Do They Really Work

Pay Me First

Tanya in Chapter VI is a real person who struggled with credit card debt while her husband Reginald, also a real person, budgeted and saved his entire life – opposites attract. During the 1970s, the average rate paid on savings accounts by financial institutions in the US was spiking. During the 1980s, when these savings accounts were paying 6 to 10%, Reginald, practicing "Pay me first," was growing his "Pay me first" account based on the interest he received his account. By the early 2000s, Reginald's account had grown to $50,000 and according to his Quicken financial software records, he was receiving between $50 and $70 in interest each month (1.5%). Today, Reginald receives .01% on his "Pay me first" account. However, when the US shut down businesses and, in most circumstances, required people to stay home to control the spread of COVID-19, Reginald's "Pay me first" savings account grew in a year by almost $4,500.00. Based on not being able to participate in budgeted activities like weekly sports and entertainment like movies and eating out, Reginald saved money.

Rewards for Sticking with "The Plan"

In June 2020, Tanya started "The Plan" to eliminate debt which is discussed in Chapter VI. Quicken Software was used to track Tanya's actual monetary transactions and as of November 30, 2021, her actual reward money looked like this:

65

Reward Money

Credit Card	Final Sched Payment	Final Bill	Leftover Interest	Purchases	Payments	Reward Money
A	$300.00	$289.42	$4.76	$69.92	$53.00	($11.10)
B	$250.00	$218.56	$0.00	$0.00	$0.00	$31.44
C	$320.00	$189.16	$3.72	$0.00	$0.00	$127.12

As explained before, reward money is the difference between the final scheduled payment and the balance owed on the final bill. Adjustments are made for leftover interest and unscheduled purchases and payments. This is a start and Tanya eliminated nearly $5,300.00 in debt in less than a year and a half.

Having Equity in Large Purchases

Reginald and Tanya purchased their first home in 1972. With 10% down payment, they were not able to avoid paying PMI; however, with appreciation in their home and timely monthly mortgage payments, they were able to eliminate PMI and pay down their mortgage sooner than their 30-year term. They purchased their second home in 1981 with no PMI required. In 1984, they opened a HELOC and purchased their first luxury vehicle (two years old) with their HELOC. Instead of "qualifying for financing," they set their own terms for paying off their vehicle. When they were ready to purchase their second luxury vehicle, they were according to plan, finished paying their HELOC loan on their first vehicle. They were never upside down in any of their vehicles. Finally in 2018 when they purchased their fourth luxury car, they decided not to purchase another luxury car with their HELOC, but to pay cash for the vehicle with the trade-in value of their third car and surplus cash they had in a slow performing investment. Reginald and Tanya took advantage of having equity in their home and cars.

The answer to "Do they work?" - Pay me First, Rewards for Savings and Having Equity in Large Purchases is yes, they do!

APPENDIX B

Credit Card Payment Schedule

Credit Card A	Finance Charge =	25.24%			
Balance Start	Monthly Finance		Balance End		Months to
of Month	Charge	Payment	of Month	Payment Due Date	Pay Balance
$1,392.99	$29.30	$202.00	$1,220.29	7/22/2020	1
$1,220.29	$25.67	$202.00	$1,043.96	8/22/2020	2
$1,043.96	$21.96	$202.00	$863.91	9/22/2020	3
$863.91	$18.17	$202.00	$680.08	10/22/2020	4
$680.08	$14.30	$202.00	$492.39	11/22/2020	5
$492.39	$10.36	$202.00	$300.75	12/22/2020	6
$300.75	$6.33	$202.00	$105.07	1/22/2021	7
$105.07	$2.21	$107.28	$0.00	2/22/2021	8
	Reward Money	$94.72			

Credit Card B	Finance Charge =	25.00%			
Balance Start	Monthly Finance		Balance End		Months to
of Month	Charge	Payment	of Month	Payment Due Date	Pay Balance
$1,818.00	$37.88	$41.00	$1,814.88	7/10/2020	1
$1,814.88	$37.81	$41.00	$1,811.68	8/10/2020	2
$1,811.68	$37.74	$41.00	$1,808.43	9/10/2020	3
$1,808.43	$37.68	$41.00	$1,805.10	10/10/2020	4
$1,805.10	$37.61	$41.00	$1,801.71	11/10/2020	5
$1,801.71	$37.54	$243.00	$1,596.25	12/10/2020	6
$1,596.25	$33.26	$243.00	$1,386.50	1/10/2021	7
$1,386.50	$28.89	$243.00	$1,172.39	2/10/2021	8
$1,172.39	$24.42	$243.00	$953.81	3/10/2021	9
$953.81	$19.87	$243.00	$730.68	4/10/2021	10
$730.68	$15.22	$243.00	$502.90	5/10/2021	11
$502.90	$10.48	$243.00	$270.38	6/10/2021	12
$270.38	$5.63	$243.00	$33.01	7/10/2021	13
$33.01	$0.69	$33.70	$0.00	8/10/2021	14

	Reward Money	$209.30			

Credit Card C	Finance Charge =	25.00%			
Balance Start of Month	Monthly Finance Charge	Payment	Balance End of Month	Payment Due Date	Months to Pay Balance
$2,088.00	$43.50	$72.00	$2,059.50	7/10/2020	1
$2,059.50	$42.91	$72.00	$2,030.41	8/10/2020	2
$2,030.41	$42.30	$72.00	$2,000.71	9/10/2020	3
$2,000.71	$41.68	$72.00	$1,970.39	10/10/2020	4
$1,970.39	$41.05	$72.00	$1,939.44	11/10/2020	5
$1,939.44	$40.40	$72.00	$1,907.84	12/10/2020	6
$1,907.84	$39.75	$72.00	$1,875.59	1/10/2021	7
$1,875.59	$39.07	$72.00	$1,842.66	2/10/2021	8
$1,842.66	$38.39	$72.00	$1,809.05	3/10/2021	9
$1,809.05	$37.69	$72.00	$1,774.74	4/10/2021	10
$1,774.74	$36.97	$72.00	$1,739.72	5/10/2021	11
$1,739.72	$36.24	$315.00	$1,460.96	6/10/2021	12
$1,460.96	$30.44	$315.00	$1,176.40	7/10/2021	13
$1,176.40	$24.51	$315.00	$885.90	8/10/2021	14
$885.90	$18.46	$315.00	$589.36	9/10/2021	15
$589.36	$12.28	$315.00	$286.64	10/10/2021	16
$286.64	$5.97	$292.61	$0.00	11/10/2021	17
	Reward Money	$22.39			

Credit Card D	Finance Charge =	25.00%			
Balance Start of Month	Monthly Finance Charge	Payment	Balance End of Month	Payment Due Date	Months to Pay Balance
$3,421.00	$71.27	$95.00	$3,397.27	7/10/2020	1
$3,397.27	$70.78	$95.00	$3,373.05	8/10/2020	2
$3,373.05	$70.27	$95.00	$3,348.32	9/10/2020	3
$3,348.32	$69.76	$95.00	$3,323.08	10/10/2020	4
$3,323.08	$69.23	$95.00	$3,297.31	11/10/2020	5
$3,297.31	$68.69	$95.00	$3,271.00	12/10/2020	6
$3,271.00	$68.15	$95.00	$3,244.15	1/10/2021	7
$3,244.15	$67.59	$95.00	$3,216.73	2/10/2021	8

Balance Start of Month	Monthly Finance Charge	Payment	Balance End of Month	Payment Due Date	Months to Pay Balance
$3,216.73	$67.02	$95.00	$3,188.75	3/10/2021	9
$3,188.75	$66.43	$95.00	$3,160.18	4/10/2021	10
$3,160.18	$65.84	$95.00	$3,131.02	5/10/2021	11
$3,131.02	$65.23	$95.00	$3,101.25	6/10/2021	12
$3,101.25	$64.61	$95.00	$3,070.86	7/10/2021	13
$3,070.86	$63.98	$95.00	$3,039.83	8/10/2021	14
$3,039.83	$63.33	$95.00	$3,008.16	9/10/2021	15
$3,008.16	$62.67	$95.00	$2,975.83	10/10/2021	16
$2,975.83	$62.00	$410.00	$2,627.83	11/10/2021	17
$2,627.83	$54.75	$410.00	$2,272.58	12/10/2021	18
$2,272.58	$47.35	$410.00	$1,909.92	1/10/2022	19
$1,909.92	$39.79	$410.00	$1,539.71	2/10/2022	20
$1,539.71	$32.08	$410.00	$1,161.79	3/10/2022	21
$1,161.79	$24.20	$410.00	$775.99	4/10/2022	22
$775.99	$16.17	$410.00	$382.16	5/10/2022	23
$382.16	$7.96	$390.12	$0.00	6/10/2022	24
	Reward Money	$19.88			

Credit Card E	Finance Charge =	25.00%			
Balance Start of Month	Monthly Finance Charge	Payment	Balance End of Month	Payment Due Date	Months to Pay Balance
$3,734.00	$77.79	$95.00	$3,716.79	7/10/2020	1
$3,716.79	$77.43	$95.00	$3,699.22	8/10/2020	2
$3,699.22	$77.07	$95.00	$3,681.29	9/10/2020	3
$3,681.29	$76.69	$95.00	$3,662.99	10/10/2020	4
$3,662.99	$76.31	$95.00	$3,644.30	11/10/2020	5
$3,644.30	$75.92	$95.00	$3,625.22	12/10/2020	6
$3,625.22	$75.53	$95.00	$3,605.75	1/10/2021	7
$3,605.75	$75.12	$95.00	$3,585.87	2/10/2021	8
$3,585.87	$74.71	$95.00	$3,565.57	3/10/2021	9
$3,565.57	$74.28	$95.00	$3,544.85	4/10/2021	10
$3,544.85	$73.85	$95.00	$3,523.71	5/10/2021	11
$3,523.71	$73.41	$95.00	$3,502.12	6/10/2021	12
$3,502.12	$72.96	$95.00	$3,480.08	7/10/2021	13
$3,480.08	$72.50	$95.00	$3,457.58	8/10/2021	14
$3,457.58	$72.03	$95.00	$3,434.61	9/10/2021	15
$3,434.61	$71.55	$95.00	$3,411.17	10/10/2021	16

$3,411.17	$71.07	$95.00	$3,387.23	11/10/2021	17
$3,387.23	$70.57	$95.00	$3,362.80	12/10/2021	18
$3,362.80	$70.06	$95.00	$3,337.86	1/10/2022	19
$3,337.86	$69.54	$95.00	$3,312.40	2/10/2022	20
$3,312.40	$69.01	$95.00	$3,286.40	3/10/2022	21
$3,286.40	$68.47	$95.00	$3,259.87	4/10/2022	22
$3,259.87	$67.91	$95.00	$3,232.78	5/10/2022	23
$3,232.78	$67.35	$505.00	$2,795.13	6/10/2022	24
$2,795.13	$58.23	$505.00	$2,348.37	7/10/2022	25
$2,348.37	$48.92	$505.00	$1,892.29	8/10/2022	26
$1,892.29	$39.42	$505.00	$1,426.71	9/10/2022	27
$1,426.71	$29.72	$505.00	$951.44	10/10/2022	28
$951.44	$19.82	$505.00	$466.26	11/10/2022	29
$466.26	$9.71	$475.97	$0.00	12/10/2022	30
	Reward Money	$29.03			

Credit Card F	Finance Charge =	25.00%			
Balance Start of Month	Monthly Finance Charge	Payment	Balance End of Month	Payment Due Date	Months to Pay Balance
$4,582.00	$95.46	$140.00	$4,537.46	7/10/2020	1
$4,537.46	$94.53	$140.00	$4,491.99	8/10/2020	2
$4,491.99	$93.58	$140.00	$4,445.57	9/10/2020	3
$4,445.57	$92.62	$140.00	$4,398.19	10/10/2020	4
$4,398.19	$91.63	$140.00	$4,349.82	11/10/2020	5
$4,349.82	$90.62	$140.00	$4,300.44	12/10/2020	6
$4,300.44	$89.59	$140.00	$4,250.03	1/10/2021	7
$4,250.03	$88.54	$140.00	$4,198.57	2/10/2021	8
$4,198.57	$87.47	$140.00	$4,146.04	3/10/2021	9
$4,146.04	$86.38	$140.00	$4,092.42	4/10/2021	10
$4,092.42	$85.26	$140.00	$4,037.68	5/10/2021	11
$4,037.68	$84.12	$140.00	$3,981.80	6/10/2021	12
$3,981.80	$82.95	$140.00	$3,924.75	7/10/2021	13
$3,924.75	$81.77	$140.00	$3,866.52	8/10/2021	14
$3,866.52	$80.55	$140.00	$3,807.07	9/10/2021	15
$3,807.07	$79.31	$140.00	$3,746.38	10/10/2021	16
$3,746.38	$78.05	$140.00	$3,684.43	11/10/2021	17
$3,684.43	$76.76	$140.00	$3,621.19	12/10/2021	18

Balance Start	Monthly Finance Charge	Payment	Balance End	Payment Due Date	Months to Pay Balance
$3,621.19	$75.44	$140.00	$3,556.63	1/10/2022	19
$3,556.63	$74.10	$140.00	$3,490.73	2/10/2022	20
$3,490.73	$72.72	$140.00	$3,423.45	3/10/2022	21
$3,423.45	$71.32	$140.00	$3,354.77	4/10/2022	22
$3,354.77	$69.89	$140.00	$3,284.67	5/10/2022	23
$3,284.67	$68.43	$140.00	$3,213.10	6/10/2022	24
$3,213.10	$66.94	$140.00	$3,140.04	7/10/2022	25
$3,140.04	$65.42	$140.00	$3,065.45	8/10/2022	26
$3,065.45	$63.86	$140.00	$2,989.32	9/10/2022	27
$2,989.32	$62.28	$140.00	$2,911.59	10/10/2022	28
$2,911.59	$60.66	$140.00	$2,832.25	11/10/2022	29
$2,832.25	$59.01	$645.00	$2,246.26	12/10/2022	30
$2,246.26	$46.80	$645.00	$1,648.05	1/10/2023	31
$1,648.05	$34.33	$645.00	$1,037.39	2/10/2023	32
$1,037.39	$21.61	$645.00	$414.00	3/10/2023	33
$414.00	$8.63	$422.63	$0.00	4/10/2023	34
Reward Money		$222.37			

Credit Card G   Finance Charge =   25.00%

Balance Start of Month	Monthly Finance Charge	Payment	Balance End of Month	Payment Due Date	Months to Pay Balance
$4,906.00	$102.21	$161.00	$4,847.21	7/10/2020	1
$4,847.21	$100.98	$161.00	$4,787.19	8/10/2020	2
$4,787.19	$99.73	$161.00	$4,725.93	9/10/2020	3
$4,725.93	$98.46	$161.00	$4,663.38	10/10/2020	4
$4,663.38	$97.15	$161.00	$4,599.54	11/10/2020	5
$4,599.54	$95.82	$161.00	$4,534.36	12/10/2020	6
$4,534.36	$94.47	$161.00	$4,467.83	1/10/2021	7
$4,467.83	$93.08	$161.00	$4,399.90	2/10/2021	8
$4,399.90	$91.66	$161.00	$4,330.57	3/10/2021	9
$4,330.57	$90.22	$161.00	$4,259.79	4/10/2021	10
$4,259.79	$88.75	$161.00	$4,187.54	5/10/2021	11
$4,187.54	$87.24	$161.00	$4,113.78	6/10/2021	12
$4,113.78	$85.70	$161.00	$4,038.48	7/10/2021	13
$4,038.48	$84.13	$161.00	$3,961.61	8/10/2021	14
$3,961.61	$82.53	$161.00	$3,883.15	9/10/2021	15
$3,883.15	$80.90	$161.00	$3,803.05	10/10/2021	16

Balance Start of Month	Monthly Finance Charge	Payment	Balance End of Month	Payment Due Date	Months to Pay Balance
$3,803.05	$79.23	$161.00	$3,721.28	11/10/2021	17
$3,721.28	$77.53	$161.00	$3,637.80	12/10/2021	18
$3,637.80	$75.79	$161.00	$3,552.59	1/10/2022	19
$3,552.59	$74.01	$161.00	$3,465.60	2/10/2022	20
$3,465.60	$72.20	$161.00	$3,376.80	3/10/2022	21
$3,376.80	$70.35	$161.00	$3,286.15	4/10/2022	22
$3,286.15	$68.46	$161.00	$3,193.62	5/10/2022	23
$3,193.62	$66.53	$161.00	$3,099.15	6/10/2022	24
$3,099.15	$64.57	$161.00	$3,002.71	7/10/2022	25
$3,002.71	$62.56	$161.00	$2,904.27	8/10/2022	26
$2,904.27	$60.51	$161.00	$2,803.78	9/10/2022	27
$2,803.78	$58.41	$161.00	$2,701.19	10/10/2022	28
$2,701.19	$56.27	$161.00	$2,596.46	11/10/2022	29
$2,596.46	$54.09	$161.00	$2,489.56	12/10/2022	30
$2,489.56	$51.87	$161.00	$2,380.42	1/10/2023	31
$2,380.42	$49.59	$161.00	$2,269.01	2/10/2023	32
$2,269.01	$47.27	$161.00	$2,155.29	3/10/2023	33
$2,155.29	$44.90	$806.00	$1,394.19	4/10/2023	34
$1,394.19	$29.05	$806.00	$617.23	5/10/2023	35
$617.23	$12.86	$630.09	$0.00	6/10/2023	36
	Reward Money	$175.91			

Credit Card H	Finance Charge =	25.00%			
Balance Start of Month	Monthly Finance Charge	Payment	Balance End of Month	Payment Due Date	Months to Pay Balance
$6,781.00	$141.27	$162.00	$6,760.27	7/10/2020	1
$6,760.27	$140.84	$162.00	$6,739.11	8/10/2020	2
$6,739.11	$140.40	$162.00	$6,717.51	9/10/2020	3
$6,717.51	$139.95	$162.00	$6,695.46	10/10/2020	4
$6,695.46	$139.49	$162.00	$6,672.94	11/10/2020	5
$6,672.94	$139.02	$162.00	$6,649.96	12/10/2020	6
$6,649.96	$138.54	$162.00	$6,626.51	1/10/2021	7
$6,626.51	$138.05	$162.00	$6,602.56	2/10/2021	8
$6,602.56	$137.55	$162.00	$6,578.11	3/10/2021	9
$6,578.11	$137.04	$162.00	$6,553.15	4/10/2021	10
$6,553.15	$136.52	$162.00	$6,527.68	5/10/2021	11
$6,527.68	$135.99	$162.00	$6,501.67	6/10/2021	12

Balance Start of Month	Monthly Finance Charge	Payment	Balance End of Month	Payment Due Date	Months to Pay Balance
$6,501.67	$135.45	$162.00	$6,475.12	7/10/2021	13
$6,475.12	$134.90	$162.00	$6,448.02	8/10/2021	14
$6,448.02	$134.33	$162.00	$6,420.36	9/10/2021	15
$6,420.36	$133.76	$162.00	$6,392.11	10/10/2021	16
$6,392.11	$133.17	$162.00	$6,363.28	11/10/2021	17
$6,363.28	$132.57	$162.00	$6,333.85	12/10/2021	18
$6,333.85	$131.96	$162.00	$6,303.81	1/10/2022	19
$6,303.81	$131.33	$162.00	$6,273.14	2/10/2022	20
$6,273.14	$130.69	$162.00	$6,241.83	3/10/2022	21
$6,241.83	$130.04	$162.00	$6,209.86	4/10/2022	22
$6,209.86	$129.37	$162.00	$6,177.24	5/10/2022	23
$6,177.24	$128.69	$162.00	$6,143.93	6/10/2022	24
$6,143.93	$128.00	$162.00	$6,109.93	7/10/2022	25
$6,109.93	$127.29	$162.00	$6,075.22	8/10/2022	26
$6,075.22	$126.57	$162.00	$6,039.78	9/10/2022	27
$6,039.78	$125.83	$162.00	$6,003.61	10/10/2022	28
$6,003.61	$125.08	$162.00	$5,966.69	11/10/2022	29
$5,966.69	$124.31	$162.00	$5,928.99	12/10/2022	30
$5,928.99	$123.52	$162.00	$5,890.51	1/10/2023	31
$5,890.51	$122.72	$162.00	$5,851.23	2/10/2023	32
$5,851.23	$121.90	$162.00	$5,811.13	3/10/2023	33
$5,811.13	$121.07	$162.00	$5,770.20	4/10/2023	34
$5,770.20	$120.21	$162.00	$5,728.41	5/10/2023	35
$5,728.41	$119.34	$968.00	$4,879.75	6/10/2023	36
$4,879.75	$101.66	$968.00	$4,013.42	7/10/2023	37
$4,013.42	$83.61	$968.00	$3,129.03	8/10/2023	38
$3,129.03	$65.19	$968.00	$2,226.22	9/10/2023	39
$2,226.22	$46.38	$968.00	$1,304.60	10/10/2023	40
$1,304.60	$27.18	$968.00	$363.77	11/10/2023	41
$363.77	$7.58	$371.35	$0.00	12/10/2023	42
	Reward Money	$596.65			

Credit Card I	Finance Charge =	25.00%			
Balance Start of Month	Monthly Finance Charge	Payment	Balance End of Month	Payment Due Date	Months to Pay Balance
$7,344.00	$153.00	$169.00	$7,328.00	7/10/2020	1
$7,328.00	$152.67	$169.00	$7,311.67	8/10/2020	2

$7,311.67	$152.33	$169.00	$7,294.99	9/10/2020	3
$7,294.99	$151.98	$169.00	$7,277.97	10/10/2020	4
$7,277.97	$151.62	$169.00	$7,260.60	11/10/2020	5
$7,260.60	$151.26	$169.00	$7,242.86	12/10/2020	6
$7,242.86	$150.89	$169.00	$7,224.75	1/10/2021	7
$7,224.75	$150.52	$169.00	$7,206.27	2/10/2021	8
$7,206.27	$150.13	$169.00	$7,187.40	3/10/2021	9
$7,187.40	$149.74	$169.00	$7,168.14	4/10/2021	10
$7,168.14	$149.34	$169.00	$7,148.47	5/10/2021	11
$7,148.47	$148.93	$169.00	$7,128.40	6/10/2021	12
$7,128.40	$148.51	$169.00	$7,107.91	7/10/2021	13
$7,107.91	$148.08	$169.00	$7,086.99	8/10/2021	14
$7,086.99	$147.65	$169.00	$7,065.63	9/10/2021	15
$7,065.63	$147.20	$169.00	$7,043.83	10/10/2021	16
$7,043.83	$146.75	$169.00	$7,021.58	11/10/2021	17
$7,021.58	$146.28	$169.00	$6,998.86	12/10/2021	18
$6,998.86	$145.81	$169.00	$6,975.67	1/10/2022	19
$6,975.67	$145.33	$169.00	$6,952.00	2/10/2022	20
$6,952.00	$144.83	$169.00	$6,927.83	3/10/2022	21
$6,927.83	$144.33	$169.00	$6,903.16	4/10/2022	22
$6,903.16	$143.82	$169.00	$6,877.98	5/10/2022	23
$6,877.98	$143.29	$169.00	$6,852.27	6/10/2022	24
$6,852.27	$142.76	$169.00	$6,826.03	7/10/2022	25
$6,826.03	$142.21	$169.00	$6,799.23	8/10/2022	26
$6,799.23	$141.65	$169.00	$6,771.89	9/10/2022	27
$6,771.89	$141.08	$169.00	$6,743.97	10/10/2022	28
$6,743.97	$140.50	$169.00	$6,715.47	11/10/2022	29
$6,715.47	$139.91	$169.00	$6,686.37	12/10/2022	30
$6,686.37	$139.30	$169.00	$6,656.67	1/10/2023	31
$6,656.67	$138.68	$169.00	$6,626.35	2/10/2023	32
$6,626.35	$138.05	$169.00	$6,595.40	3/10/2023	33
$6,595.40	$137.40	$169.00	$6,563.80	4/10/2023	34
$6,563.80	$136.75	$169.00	$6,531.55	5/10/2023	35
$6,531.55	$136.07	$169.00	$6,498.62	6/10/2023	36
$6,498.62	$135.39	$169.00	$6,465.01	7/10/2023	37
$6,465.01	$134.69	$169.00	$6,430.70	8/10/2023	38
$6,430.70	$133.97	$169.00	$6,395.67	9/10/2023	39
$6,395.67	$133.24	$169.00	$6,359.92	10/10/2023	40

Balance Start	Monthly Finance Charge	Payment	Balance End	Payment Due Date	Months to Pay Balance
$6,359.92	$132.50	$1,137.00	$5,355.41	11/10/2023	41
$5,355.41	$111.57	$1,137.00	$4,329.99	12/10/2023	42
$4,329.99	$90.21	$1,137.00	$3,283.19	1/10/2024	43
$3,283.19	$68.40	$1,137.00	$2,214.59	2/10/2024	44
$2,214.59	$46.14	$1,137.00	$1,123.73	3/10/2024	45
$1,123.73	$23.41	$1,137.00	$10.14	4/10/2024	46
$10.14	$0.21	$10.35	$0.00	5/10/2024	47
	Reward Money	$1,126.65			

Credit Card J	Finance Charge =	25.00%			
Balance Start of Month	Monthly Finance Charge	Payment	Balance End of Month	Payment Due Date	Months to Pay Balance
$10,380.00	$216.25	$316.00	$10,280.25	7/10/2020	1
$10,280.25	$214.17	$316.00	$10,178.42	8/10/2020	2
$10,178.42	$212.05	$316.00	$10,074.47	9/10/2020	3
$10,074.47	$209.88	$316.00	$9,968.36	10/10/2020	4
$9,968.36	$207.67	$316.00	$9,860.03	11/10/2020	5
$9,860.03	$205.42	$316.00	$9,749.45	12/10/2020	6
$9,749.45	$203.11	$316.00	$9,636.56	1/10/2021	7
$9,636.56	$200.76	$316.00	$9,521.32	2/10/2021	8
$9,521.32	$198.36	$316.00	$9,403.68	3/10/2021	9
$9,403.68	$195.91	$316.00	$9,283.59	4/10/2021	10
$9,283.59	$193.41	$316.00	$9,161.00	5/10/2021	11
$9,161.00	$190.85	$316.00	$9,035.86	6/10/2021	12
$9,035.86	$188.25	$316.00	$8,908.10	7/10/2021	13
$8,908.10	$185.59	$316.00	$8,777.69	8/10/2021	14
$8,777.69	$182.87	$316.00	$8,644.56	9/10/2021	15
$8,644.56	$180.09	$316.00	$8,508.65	10/10/2021	16
$8,508.65	$177.26	$316.00	$8,369.92	11/10/2021	17
$8,369.92	$174.37	$316.00	$8,228.29	12/10/2021	18
$8,228.29	$171.42	$316.00	$8,083.71	1/10/2022	19
$8,083.71	$168.41	$316.00	$7,936.12	2/10/2022	20
$7,936.12	$165.34	$316.00	$7,785.46	3/10/2022	21
$7,785.46	$162.20	$316.00	$7,631.66	4/10/2022	22
$7,631.66	$158.99	$316.00	$7,474.65	5/10/2022	23
$7,474.65	$155.72	$316.00	$7,314.37	6/10/2022	24
$7,314.37	$152.38	$316.00	$7,150.75	7/10/2022	25

Balance Start of Month	Monthly Finance Charge	Payment	Balance End of Month	Payment Due Date	Months to Pay Balance
$7,150.75	$148.97	$316.00	$6,983.73	8/10/2022	26
$6,983.73	$145.49	$316.00	$6,813.22	9/10/2022	27
$6,813.22	$141.94	$316.00	$6,639.16	10/10/2022	28
$6,639.16	$138.32	$316.00	$6,461.48	11/10/2022	29
$6,461.48	$134.61	$316.00	$6,280.09	12/10/2022	30
$6,280.09	$130.84	$316.00	$6,094.93	1/10/2023	31
$6,094.93	$126.98	$316.00	$5,905.91	2/10/2023	32
$5,905.91	$123.04	$316.00	$5,712.95	3/10/2023	33
$5,712.95	$119.02	$316.00	$5,515.97	4/10/2023	34
$5,515.97	$114.92	$316.00	$5,314.88	5/10/2023	35
$5,314.88	$110.73	$316.00	$5,109.61	6/10/2023	36
$5,109.61	$106.45	$316.00	$4,900.06	7/10/2023	37
$4,900.06	$102.08	$316.00	$4,686.14	8/10/2023	38
$4,686.14	$97.63	$316.00	$4,467.77	9/10/2023	39
$4,467.77	$93.08	$316.00	$4,244.85	10/10/2023	40
$4,244.85	$88.43	$316.00	$4,017.29	11/10/2023	41
$4,017.29	$83.69	$316.00	$3,784.98	12/10/2023	42
$3,784.98	$78.85	$316.00	$3,547.83	1/10/2024	43
$3,547.83	$73.91	$316.00	$3,305.75	2/10/2024	44
$3,305.75	$68.87	$316.00	$3,058.62	3/10/2024	45
$3,058.62	$63.72	$1,453.00	$1,669.34	4/10/2024	46
$1,669.34	$34.78	$1,453.00	$251.11	5/10/2024	47
$251.11	$5.23	$256.35	$0.00	6/10/2024	48
	Reward Money	$1,196.65			

| Credit Card K | Finance Charge = | 25.00% | | | |
Balance Start of Month	Monthly Finance Charge	Payment	Balance End of Month	Payment Due Date	Months to Pay Balance
$11,336.00	$236.17	$334.00	$11,238.17	7/10/2020	1
$11,238.17	$234.13	$334.00	$11,138.30	8/10/2020	2
$11,138.30	$232.05	$334.00	$11,036.34	9/10/2020	3
$11,036.34	$229.92	$334.00	$10,932.27	10/10/2020	4
$10,932.27	$227.76	$334.00	$10,826.02	11/10/2020	5
$10,826.02	$225.54	$334.00	$10,717.56	12/10/2020	6
$10,717.56	$223.28	$334.00	$10,606.85	1/10/2021	7
$10,606.85	$220.98	$334.00	$10,493.82	2/10/2021	8
$10,493.82	$218.62	$334.00	$10,378.44	3/10/2021	9

$10,378.44	$216.22	$334.00	$10,260.66	4/10/2021	10
$10,260.66	$213.76	$334.00	$10,140.43	5/10/2021	11
$10,140.43	$211.26	$334.00	$10,017.68	6/10/2021	12
$10,017.68	$208.70	$334.00	$9,892.39	7/10/2021	13
$9,892.39	$206.09	$334.00	$9,764.48	8/10/2021	14
$9,764.48	$203.43	$334.00	$9,633.90	9/10/2021	15
$9,633.90	$200.71	$334.00	$9,500.61	10/10/2021	16
$9,500.61	$197.93	$334.00	$9,364.54	11/10/2021	17
$9,364.54	$195.09	$334.00	$9,225.63	12/10/2021	18
$9,225.63	$192.20	$334.00	$9,083.84	1/10/2022	19
$9,083.84	$189.25	$334.00	$8,939.08	2/10/2022	20
$8,939.08	$186.23	$334.00	$8,791.31	3/10/2022	21
$8,791.31	$183.15	$334.00	$8,640.47	4/10/2022	22
$8,640.47	$180.01	$334.00	$8,486.47	5/10/2022	23
$8,486.47	$176.80	$334.00	$8,329.28	6/10/2022	24
$8,329.28	$173.53	$334.00	$8,168.80	7/10/2022	25
$8,168.80	$170.18	$334.00	$8,004.99	8/10/2022	26
$8,004.99	$166.77	$334.00	$7,837.76	9/10/2022	27
$7,837.76	$163.29	$334.00	$7,667.04	10/10/2022	28
$7,667.04	$159.73	$334.00	$7,492.77	11/10/2022	29
$7,492.77	$156.10	$334.00	$7,314.87	12/10/2022	30
$7,314.87	$152.39	$334.00	$7,133.27	1/10/2023	31
$7,133.27	$148.61	$334.00	$6,947.88	2/10/2023	32
$6,947.88	$144.75	$334.00	$6,758.62	3/10/2023	33
$6,758.62	$140.80	$334.00	$6,565.43	4/10/2023	34
$6,565.43	$136.78	$334.00	$6,368.21	5/10/2023	35
$6,368.21	$132.67	$334.00	$6,166.88	6/10/2023	36
$6,166.88	$128.48	$334.00	$5,961.36	7/10/2023	37
$5,961.36	$124.19	$334.00	$5,751.55	8/10/2023	38
$5,751.55	$119.82	$334.00	$5,537.37	9/10/2023	39
$5,537.37	$115.36	$334.00	$5,318.74	10/10/2023	40
$5,318.74	$110.81	$334.00	$5,095.54	11/10/2023	41
$5,095.54	$106.16	$334.00	$4,867.70	12/10/2023	42
$4,867.70	$101.41	$334.00	$4,635.11	1/10/2024	43
$4,635.11	$96.56	$334.00	$4,397.68	2/10/2024	44
$4,397.68	$91.62	$334.00	$4,155.29	3/10/2024	45
$4,155.29	$86.57	$334.00	$3,907.86	4/10/2024	46
$3,907.86	$81.41	$1,787.00	$2,202.28	5/10/2024	47

$2,202.28	$45.88	$1,787.00	$461.16	6/10/2024	48
$461.16	$9.61	$470.76	$0.00	7/10/2024	49
	Reward Money	$1,316.24			
	Grand Total Reward	$5,009.78			

APPENDIX C
Index

APPENDIX D

Bibliography

Bureau of Statistics Consumer Expenditures Survey 2019

Carnevale, Rose and Cheah, Georgetown University Center on Education and the Workforce, "The College Payoff."

Chase Bank, chase.com, "What is PMI and How is it calculated?"

Clark, Cecilia; Helhoski, Anna, June 2, 2021, Nerdwallet, "Are Student Loans Worth It? A College Affordability Calculator."

Experian Credit Reporting Bureau, third quarter 2018

Friedman, Zack, February 20, 2021, Forbes, "Student Loan Debt Statistics In 2021: Record $1.7 Trillion.

Marquand, Barbara, August 13, 2020, Nerdwallet, "Tips for First-Time Home Buyer."

National Association of Colleges and Employers Staff Writer, "Average Salary for Class of 2019 up almost 6 percent over Class of 2018's," September 4, 2020.

The Holy Bible New King James Version, c 1982 Thomas Nelson, Inc.

Wikipedia, Home Equity Line of Credit

Zillow.com, "Home Affordability Calculator"

ABOUT THE AUTHOR

Ronald George Lucas, Sr was born and raised in Washington, DC. He was educated in the DC Public Schools, Bell Elementary, Browne Junior High and Eastern High. Lucas graduated with a Bachelor of Science Degree in Mechanical Engineering in 1971 from Howard University. His financial career started in high school as President and Treasurer of his high school fraternity and continued in adult life as Treasurer of the Board of Directors for Resources Federal Credit Union, Treasurer/Chairman of Finance Committee of Grace United Methodist Church and President/Chief Financial Officer of VIP Travel Agency. Before retiring from Federal Energy Regulatory Commission (FERC) in 2003, Lucas worked over 30 years as an expert witness testifying in rate cases requiring engineering, cost of service, rate design and depreciation analyses. Lucas testified in over 30 cases involving interstate gas, electric and oil companies, including Market Manipulation in California in Docket No. EL02-113-000, El Paso Electric Company, Enron Power Marketing, Inc. Enron Capital and Trade Resources Corporation. As a consultant after retiring from FERC, Lucas worked several years at Brown, Williams, Moorhead & Quinn, Inc, Energy Consultants where his largest client was Chevron Pipeline Company.

Over the course of his career, Lucas presented technical papers related to depreciation in cost of service studies before the Iowa State Regulatory Conference in 1982 and before the Annual Meeting of the Society of Depreciation Professionals in 1992. Lucas has also written articles published in the Journal of the Society of Depreciation Professionals and participated in the preparation of the National Association of Regulatory Commissioners' reprint of its text, "Public Utility Depreciation Practices," August 1996.

Lucas' financial background includes budgeting and forecasting financial requirements of Resources Federal Credit Union as a member and later Treasurer of the Board of Directors of that credit union. Duties as Treasurer and later Chairman of Finance

Committee for Grace United Methodist Church included preparing the church budget, paying bills and salaries of church staff. As president/Chief Financial Officer of VIP Travel Agency, Lucas prepared budgets, payroll and paid expenses for the agency.

Lucas is a tithing member of the First Baptist Church of Glenarden and has been married over 50 years to his college sweetheart, Malcine McGriff Lucas. Their family consists of adult children Chuck, Ron, Jr., Dana and Derek and 10 grandchildren.